HITLER
went to
HEAVEN

David Dunning

Copyright © 2013 David Dunning

All rights reserved.

ISBN: 0615908810

ISBN-13: 978-0615908816

INSPIRED BY

My wife and two boys. Doo-wop music. A road trip. Ice cold Coca Cola in glass bottles. My parents. Coffee. The beach. The IRS. Evangelical Christians. Burritos with french fries inside them. Doctors. Classic cars. Our Government. My siblings. Surfboards. Mormon missionaries. Money. The Mayan calendar. My close friends. The sunset. Time.

LOVE.

THE GUTS

Inspiration

A Proper Introduction   1

Resume   6

Education   9

Religion   15

Lifestyle   22

Health   26

Money   31

In a Nutshell   37

1 A PROPER INTRODUCTION

Let's get one thing straight, Adolf Hitler was an asshole. This book is not about him. However, this book is about an idea as controversial as his socially retarded Nazis. Hitler went to heaven and I'll tell you why.

We live in a world of priests, pastors and gurus of every conceivable religion, philosophy, lifestyle and fad. They all have a direct telephone line to God and a BMW. We hang onto their words and wisdom desperate for salvation and blessing. We attend their meetings, give them our money, and follow their rules. We praise ourselves, belittle others and gloat in our own self-righteous glory.

I want you to try something. Repeat this

sentence: "I am not a (insert your religion/faith)." Now do it again. How badly did that hurt? Was there a knot in your stomach that urged you to stop before it was too late? If not, then congratulations you have an ability that most scholars have long assumed extinct. Critical thought.

Whoa, stop the bus. Critical thought? We can wrap our heads around throwing a thousand Jewish human beings into an oven, but critical thought about our own religion or ideology? I know I'm asking a lot, but that's where this will get good. Let's break it down even further.

In every direction that you turn there are billboards and blow horns screaming at you to follow them. Promising everything from a one way ticket to heaven, life longevity, and even a larger penis. In spite of these claims, how many people do you know of that have lived until the age of 200? How many people do you know that have never gotten the flu after a flu shot? How many people do you know of that you can tell me exactly where they went when they died?

That last question is important. You don't know any. That's right, you have absolutely no idea where anyone has gone when they died. Yet still, like blind fighter pilots, we stand around debating whether or not our fallen comrades have gone to see a bearded man with a stick, or a circus clown with horns. It is as stupid as it sounds.

Don't close this book yet. I know that last comment hurt. It wasn't meant to, and it is not a statement of hopelessness. I believe in God. Our definitions may be different, but stick with me. If you're really as devoted of an (insert your religion/faith), you shouldn't have any problem anyhow because you already know the secret to our existence. On the other hand, if you're intrigued even just for the sake of argument, then please continue on. I value your opinion and think you may actually have something to contribute to humanity.

This book isn't just about religion and faith. Most importantly this book is about you. It is about your life and the decisions that you make each and every moment. I want to know why. More importantly I want you to ask yourself why? What are your choices being influenced by? Who put what ideas where? Is being vegan really going to make you a better person? Does God really care if you wear special underwear, a cloth, or a napkin on your head? I want us to challenge ourselves because it is the only true path to evolution.

We live in a constant state of miracle.

Every single split second is an awe inspiring, jaw dropping moment. Unfortunately, we've been robbed of that awareness. Rarely does anyone ever stop to really think about what exactly is going on.

Everyday realities as common as a caterpillar becoming an entirely new creature, or asking yourself "What the hell is the internet, really?" Never get discussed. You're thinking to yourself right now that this is nothing new, and there is no reason to change things as they are. You're wrong. You have the potential for a divine, heroic, and abundant adventure.

This book is about freedom, truth, and love. You are born with those three inherent rights, and no human being should ever arrogantly try and stomp on them. Nobody on this earth, and I will repeat that, nobody on this earth deserves anything anymore than you do. God is not some juvenile running a standardized testing clinic in an upstairs office.

You are infinitesimal, yet infinite. Wrap your head around the idea that just as a single drop of water goes into the ocean, it becomes the entire ocean. I'll go a step further. Consider that we are all made of the same universal fabric that makes up all of Creation. We are all a part of God, therefore is it possible that you are God? I am not telling you for certain that you are, but again, you cannot tell me for certain that you aren't.

It is gut check time. Many of you are calling this a blasphemy already. Your insides burn with fear at the idea of possibly not having it all figured out. Could your tithe money have been wasted? Was your decision to circumcise based upon a few thousand year old fairy tale? Are the gays really getting married?

Life is a beautiful thing. Let's not waste it trying to be perfect.

2 MY RESUME

Before we dive into this, I need to tell you something. I am absolutely, 100 percent unqualified to write this book. We all are, that's the beauty of it. The true insanity is how amazingly well some individuals have developed their talents of deception and sales. They have entire congregations and groups of people believing that they actually know what is best for them, more than the people do themselves.

Here is what I do have on my side and why you should listen. I am exactly like you. In my life up until this point, I have worn many hats: student, airman, bartender, realtor, musician, landscaper, aviation technician, husband and father. I work hard and am a badass at most all of these things.

I have also stumbled with many issues. When I was younger I would do almost anything for a laugh and was a little shy around the girls. I was a late bloomer. I have always cared a little too much about what other people thought. I have a temper and curse like a lesbian sailor. I can be shallow and struggle with empathy. However, I am also generous, loving, and genuinely want those around me to be comfortable and happy. The bottom line is that I am far from perfect and so are you.

It is in this state of imperfection that we must band together. We have to sound the horn, rally the troops and rebel. Rebel against false idols, unrealistic expectations, and a socio-economic system built upon ideas and things that are not even real.

The greatest illusion of all is that the issues that we struggle with are "complicated." They are not. They are not even close to complicated. They are so stupidly simple that most children can find solutions for them in between recess and their potty break. It is only as adults that we choose to create a complicated issue with a thousand variables that seems to have no end in sight. This book is not long because it doesn't have to be.

The point is this, despite our perceived imperfections, we all have the amazing ability to make our lives great. It doesn't take a guru, a Gandhi or a Christ to change the world. It takes you, pulling your head out of your ass and waking up to your own right to be here and enjoy every single second of it.

3 EDUCATION

"Everybody is a genius. But if you judge a fish by its ability to climb a tree, it will live its whole life believing that it is stupid."

— Albert Einstein

Let me tell you a little known fact. You were born destined for greatness. Now, let me tell you a secret. You were bred for mediocrity. From the first moment you strapped on a backpack, you were taught one thing. Be like everyone else. Now, no one will admit to this, especially not the teachers, administrators and policy makers. We like to gloss over this fact with a few pitiful ethnic appreciation days, a sack race, and a gold star.

Remember how I said that none of the issues

that tether us to a life less than we deserve are complicated? This is one of them. There is a very simple solution to this, and that is to create geniuses. Each and every one of us has different strengths. There is no such thing as a "weakness." There are only subjects and ideas that you do not give a shit about. There is nothing inherently wrong with that.

A simple idea I read about in Deepak Chopra's, *The Seven Spiritual Laws for Parents* is in the following example. Lets suppose you are stellar at math, but can't tell the difference between a Bunsen burner and a #2 pencil in chemistry. Our education system's knee jerk reaction is for you to get a tutor in chemistry and bring you up to some abstract normal level of knowledge. This is wrong. You need a math tutor, someone to grow your natural talent to its maximum capacity. Ditch the chemistry. Become a genius in math.

The world does not need millions of mediocre doctors, scientists, teachers, entrepreneurs and athletes. We need geniuses that light their respective field on fire each and every day because they are great at it. There is absolutely no point in requiring every human being to learn a standardized amount of generally useless information.

What exists now is a bullshit method of ignoring individual talents and highlighting areas of disinterest. We have effectively suffocated our own inner light and put out the fire. Again, if you are good at math, be great at math. It is your right to say, "I don't give a damn about chemistry and am probably terrible at dodge ball. Therefore, I do not need to waste my time watching paint peel in either of those classrooms."

A logical question would be, "What am I great at?" or "How do I find out what my child is naturally gifted in?" The answer is radical - playtime. You find out what you are great at when you are playing and having fun. This is when your natural talents, your imagination, and your enthusiasm for life are on steroids. What you choose to do on your own, and have fun doing is what you are great at.

Of course, there are variables that some jackass will always try and argue with me about. For example, what if I live, eat, dream, and love basketball, but am 4 foot 7 inches tall and weigh 135 pounds wet (this was me in middle school, by the way). Be creative. Be smart. Maybe your chances of being drafted by the Lakers are slim, but who says you cannot be a world-class coach, an Olympic trainer or even an NBA broadcaster. The point is to involve your passions in what you do everyday, and you will be great at it.

    This may appear idealistic and impossible on the surface, but it is not. It is actually common sense. The reason it appears to be impossible is because the infrastructure for this current idiotic method of education is so large and set in place.

    At this moment, your alternative options are homeschool or a specialized private institution. Private school generally comes with a cost and a shitty uniform. The really cool private schools that cater to specific skill sets often times operate on a lottery system for admission. If you find one that works, go for it.

    "Homeschool" has become a bad word amongst most suburban, well-trained and obedient families. I want you to know that homeschool does not breed social lepers. Bad parents breed social lepers. Homeschool can be one of the greatest educations that a child can achieve.

    Personalized lessons, practical applications, and the freedom to explore are second to none in a homeschool environment. Maybe instead of memorizing the Pythagorean theorem, because God knows we all use that shit every day, your child could learn how to cook a proper meal, balance a checkbook and change their own car's oil. Amazingly the end product would be a self sufficient, confident adult that knows who they are. I am not saying that homeschool is the ultimate answer here, but clearly what we have going on is not working as advertised.

Think about it. Under the current system, every 18-year-old runs off to college to try and find themselves. It's usually at the bottom of a cheap bottle of vodka. We send ourselves off into adulthood essentially equipped with our underwear and some lunch money. It's ludicrous. You just spent the last 18 years of your life being educated, yet you can't work the coin operated laundry machine at the end of the hall. Goddamn genius.

It is exposure that is important. Exposure grants us the opportunity to find ourselves in places that we may never have thought possible. Broaden your child's perspective by giving them every chance possible to try something new. Next, step back and watch them take off as they learn to teach you something.

Finally, while we are dismantling the current educational shithouse, I can impart only one critical piece of advice. Ask questions. Textbooks are just that, books with text in them. Another imperfect human being, within an entirely imperfect system wrote them. Let's remember that the earth was once officially flat. If history has taught us anything, it is that we have been wrong more times than we would like to admit.

Most everything you are taught is a theory. Some of them more tested than others, but generally theories. For every theory that you are taught, consider what would be if the opposite of the theory were true. Case in point, what if the earth were hollow? Go down that rabbit hole, and tell the world what you find. We all might just learn something.

4 RELIGION

"The whole history of these books [the Gospels] is so defective and doubtful that it seems vain to attempt minute enquiry into it: and such tricks have been played with their text, and with the texts of other books relating to them, that we have a right, from that cause, to entertain much doubt what parts of them are genuine. In the New Testament there is internal evidence that parts of it have proceeded from an extraordinary man; and that other parts are of the fabric of very inferior minds. It is as easy to separate those parts, as to pick out diamonds from dunghills."

—Thomas Jefferson, letter to John Adams, January 24, 1814

Since the beginning of recorded history, we have been killing, torturing, judging, and yes, even molesting each other in the name of God.

It doesn't get much further from divinity than that. In the never ending pissing contest for who knows God the best, we have become so arrogant as to take the position that we have God figured out.

We think we know exactly what we have to do in order to earn the golden ticket. Life is presented to us as one long multiple-choice test in order to determine whether or not we get to eat cake for an eternity or get thrown into a fire. Seriously, I am embarrassed for anyone who believes this.

How offensive it must be to God that we have painted such a poor, juvenile, and ugly picture of the Creator. The source of all of Creation. Every atom and molecule that forms and shapes itself into something magnificent, we have decided is actually just a vengeful old man who is capable of petty human emotions.

You are probably judging me right now, afraid that I may have struck even a small chord of truth. You are probably thinking that I just need to be saved and that a heavy dose of Jesus is the cure. You may even question at this point if I need to skip Jesus and head straight to the principal himself.

Let me tell you one thing. The Jesus that I choose to believe may have existed, would be dunking your head in a toilet right about now. He'd call you an arrogant bastard, and then he and I would go and have a beer with his hooker girlfriend. You're only getting angrier with me now at my presumption that his girlfriend was a hooker. You know why? Because you're judging her too. That my friend, is the exact problem with religion. You think you actually know.

Additionally, it strikes me as a little strange that Jesus apparently disappeared into his bedroom for the first 30 years of his life. I mean, supposedly, historical record is so accurate as to know that Jesus received some cheap cologne and salt and pepper on his birthday. So then why the blank slate for ninety percent of his life?

If we knew at birth that he was going to be such an influential figure, I would have expected the paparazzi to have been outside that dirty little manger with their stone tablets chiseling out his every word.

Following this theme of critical thinking, let me ask another very basic question regarding the Bible. In the beginning there was Adam and Eve, the two human beings whom we are all to have descended from. They initially had two sons named Cain and Abel.

In a great turn of events, Cain murdered his

brother Abel and was forced into exile. Juvenile detention had not yet been created. Somewhere between leaving his parents front doorstep and the Neverland Ranch, Cain found a wife. Stop right there. He found an adult wife. From where? I thought that Adam and Eve got this party started. Apparently they had neighbors.

I am not the first person to ask these questions. I am not saying that the Bible is a book to be disregarded. However, I am saying that if your story starts out with more questions than a two year old on a road trip, you may need to take it for what it is. A collection of fairy tales. Some of them with moral merit, some of them with an interesting ending, and a couple of them might even be true.

The Gospels evidently began being written and gathered over 40 years after Jesus' passing. Let me ask you, how well can you remember an event 10 years ago let alone 40? Add to that over 3,000 years of interpretation, manipulation, and editing and you've got about as solid of a foundation as a mud hut. If at this point you exclaim, "Well nobody's ever changed a word in the Bible!" Please put this book down right now. You are an idiot.

I am picking on Christianity at the moment. However, the absurdity of blind faith is an inescapable reality of all religions. We study the lives of and preoccupy ourselves with the teachings of a bunch of dead men. Why not look towards the living instead for some guidance?

Look at the daily miracle of a sunset, the evolution of a cluster of cells in a woman's womb, or the way that a good song can make you feel. There are glimpses into the divine in every direction you turn. This world and the universe are incredible even in their most basic state of existence.

There is no competition to be had in regard to religion and spirituality. There is not one true path toward enlightenment and eternal happiness. There is simply the here and now. It does not matter whether or not the great teachers of our religions actually existed. It does not change the here and now.

If you were to find out that your religious idol were simply a character in a book, it would have absolutely no affect upon your immediate circumstances. You would still be you, and waking up every morning would not be any less of an adventure.

We do not need religion in order to instill a sense of morality within ourselves. We need only look to each other to recognize what serves the greater of humanity for the good. If you were the only individual on earth, there would be no such thing as morality. You could not commit a wrong against yourself. Your actions would simply be a choice you had made. However, in the presence of other human beings, we introduce the idea of right and wrong. It is not a difficult road to travel. Simply put, treat others as you would like to be treated.

Hitler went to Heaven, because it is the only other place to go.

Let me break it down for you as simply as I know how. There are two rooms that we all live in. The alive room, and the dead room. We all come through one door and leave out another. We don't know what is in the dead room, yet we spend our lives blindly describing what we think is on the other side of the door.

We are like children with blindfolds on and our ears pressed against a cup on a wall. We bicker over who knows best what is on the other side. Do not waste your time attempting to map out the unknown. You will never succeed. The alive room is begging for you to take a look around. Live free of judgment and fear. God and Creation are too great to waste their own energy playing games with you.

Faith is a powerful tool. Faith can get us through the most trying of times and give us strength in the moments when we need it the most. Have faith. Have faith in a Creation that is undeniably bigger than us. There is excitement and wonder when you choose to accept that you live in the unknown. Have faith in the magic that weaves its way throughout our lives. Have faith in knowing that when you separate Creation from the crude definitions afforded by religion, you allow this existence to blossom fully into all that it is ever destined to be. Most importantly, have faith in knowing that there is no one out there any closer to God than you are. Have faith in yourself.

5 LIFESTYLE

"I might not be the same, but that's not important. No freedom 'til we're equal, damn right I support it."

– Macklemore

Somewhere, right this moment, two men are having sex with each other. In another part of the world, there is a man living with his 3 wives. To top it off, your neighbor just smoked a joint with his wife. Scary. Now look around you, has anything changed? Has the world, as you know it come crumbling down around your fragile ego? No, get over it.

There are people in the world that choose to do things a little differently than you do. As long as it doesn't get in the way of your mundane TV dinner and jeopardy lifestyle, then really, what does it matter?

The comedy here is in the fact that the ignorant public fights these ideas and actions as if they are fighting off some three-headed monster that has not yet arrived. As if by screaming like a jackass on a street corner, or by preaching discrimination and hate, that they can actually stop these things from happening.

I hate to be the bearer of bad news to these folks, but that ship has sailed. In fact, there is probably a gay man, with three wives, smoking pot right now reading this book. These people and issues have always been, and always will be a part of this reality on earth. Accept that fact and you can save yourself a mild stroke when you begin seeing letters addressed to, "Mr. and Mr. John Doe."

You are born to be you, and you have a right to explore every version of you that exists. We take ourselves so seriously that the idea of anyone choosing to be anything other than a carbon copy of you is terrifying. You are shaken to your core. You ask yourself why? Why would anyone choose to do anything any differently than I do? It doesn't make sense. The fear of the unknown turns into a disgusting display of hatred, bigotry, judgment and division.

We tend to define each other by the choices we make rather than the fiber of our character. If an individual chooses not to eat meat, they fall into the category of that type of person. If an individual smokes cigarettes, then they are another type of person. If a man chooses to wear a dress on the weekends, he is an entirely other type of person.

While these choices may reflect certain interests or values, the bottom line remains the same. Strip away the clothes, attitudes, and everyday masks, and you are left with something profound. A mirror image of yourself. Naked, empowered, and having arrived through the same front door as everyone else.

This is not an endorsement for throwing morality out the window and behaving recklessly through desire. We must always be conscious of how our actions impact the others around us. However, if what one man or woman chooses to do in their life has absolutely no bearing upon your daily ritual, why in the hell should it concern you? It doesn't.

Taking into consideration that there are nearly 7 billion human beings on this earth, for you to take the conceited position of passing judgment upon all others unlike you is the greatest blasphemy of them all. Move on with your life, do something better with your time and stop arguing about your interpretation of what God says is ok. I am remotely certain that God can handle those matters without our assistance. I am even more certain that God is too great to give a damn one way or another.

Celebrate our differences. Without these differences the world would be one giant suburb. We all have something to offer, and in turn we need to learn how to receive. There is nothing to fight about. Live and let live, love and let love, and above all else enjoy the ride for yourself. It's that cool.

6 HEALTH

"I don't have an on-season and off-season training- I'm training for life."

- Laird Hamilton

I was at the grocery store when I spotted my family's new doctor parking their mini-van in the fire lane of the store entrance. I wondered what the emergency was. The answer soon emerged when the driver's side door swung open. The educated M.D. heaved their morbidly obese body out of the vehicle and casually waddled into the store.

Now it made sense. Dr. "12 piece chicken dinner" had parked in the fire lane in order to avoid the 50-yard walk from the designated parking spaces. I thought to myself, "This blimp is a doctor for children." Welcome to healthcare in America.

To be fair, once inside the store, I am sure that the doctor made the conscious decision and opted for the diet soda. My point is that clearly this educated and esteemed Doctor can't take care of step one in regard to their own physical health. Consequently, they have absolutely no business giving healthcare guidance to anyone else for as long as they are wearing clothing sized for farm animals.

That may seem harsh, but lets call a spade a spade here. If you are obese, you either do not care enough about your own well being to make a change, or you are uneducated in all things healthy. Both options are a piss poor choice for a doctor. I mean that with love.

It is this backwards mentality that has permeated most every aspect of what we have come to know and expect of healthcare and longevity in America. The scary part is that it goes even deeper and gets even darker than just obesity.

There is an entire book of material that could be, and is written about each one of the following topics. I am trusting you to dig deeper on your own.

Lets begin with birth. Do you know how many vaccinations were given to infants in the

1950's? My father had zero. He is still alive. Do you know how many vaccinations I received as an infant in 1983? I was given six. Do you know how many vaccinations my son's doctors would like to administer to him today? Over 30 doses of 14 different vaccines by the age of two. Today more American children are developing Autism than ever before in history.

There is a specialized federal court in place, referred to simply as Vaccine Court that handles any claims of damages caused by vaccines. It is officially known as the Office of Special Masters of the U.S. Court of Federal Claims. There is no jury present. Interesting provision to be made for such a noble field. This court awarded two families upwards of $1 million dollars in January of 2013 for damages caused by, and linked to the development of autism in separate cases. Do your research. Ask questions.

Let's move on. The water you drink, bathe in, and flush down the toilet is full of chemicals. This is a fact. Fluoride is one of them. Your toothpaste label warns that you must contact poison control immediately in the event that more than a pea sized amount is swallowed. This is not because of the bubble gum flavor. It is due to the presence of fluoride.

There is the same amount of fluoride in an 8oz glass of tap water as there is in the pea-sized dose of toothpaste. It is a poison. Now, there is logically no way to regulate fluoride dosage in drinking water due to the simple fact that everyone drinks different amounts of water. Ninety seven percent of Europe has banned the fluoridation of drinking water. What are we missing here? Do the research. Ask questions.

Finally, lets talk about food. Diet seems to be a volatile topic of conversation. Like religion, most everyone blindly claims to have it figured out. Let me just make note of the following:

- The tomato on your fast food chicken sandwich does not fulfill your body's need for vegetables.
- Perhaps, it is not the presence of meat and dairy in a diet that causes health ailments, as much as it may be the absence of fruits and vegetables.
- Read your ingredient labels. If you cannot pronounce it, then it is not food.
- Eat well, eat often, and eat real food.
- Make sustainable choices that are as close

to the source as possible.
- The food you eat literally makes up a large part of the composition of your body. Wouldn't it make sense then that a healthy diet that includes whole foods, fruits and vegetables is paramount to your health even more-so than modern medicine?

Your body truly is a temple. It houses the soul that is reading these words this very second. Your health is your greatest gift to yourself and the people that you love. Prepare your body for the adventure of life, and it will not let you down when you need it the most.

7 MONEY

> *"I know you got 40 billion dollars, but can you just keep it to one house? You only need ONE house. And if you only got two kids, can you just keep it to two rooms? I mean why have 52 rooms and you know there's somebody with no room?! It just don't make sense to me. It don't."*
>
> *— Tupac Shakur*

We need to stop lying to ourselves. Admit to the fact that money, whether it be the pursuit of, hatred toward, or lack of, has come to rule our lives. It is the greatest and most cruel practical joke ever played upon humanity. It determines our opportunities, healthcare, entertainment, and ability to get laid. It needs to be redefined.

If you are like most of the population, by

the time that you retire you will have spent twice the amount of time in your carpool and cubicle than you will have spent with your spouse, children, family and friends. You were not created for the purpose of earning a paycheck. Your life is your own to do with what you please.

We have created a system based upon a fraudulent paper placeholder. You are literally enslaved to this toilet paper equivalent in order to receive the most basic of God given rights. The fact of the matter is that abundance is your birthright.

Look at the stars. Look at the moon. Look at the grass growing in your yard. Watch a child playing in the waves of the ocean. Look at a fucking sea horse. Now tell me what kind of sense it would make that the Universe would exist for the purpose of you needing to worry about collecting paper tokens in order to eat, drink, and be taken care of.

Then, just to kick you in the balls, you get robbed of upwards of 30 percent of your magic tree paper in the form of taxes. Some of you truly believe that this tax revenue all goes towards paving roads and paying firemen. If that is an illusion you choose to endure, I suspect that you also still wait for Kris

Kringle to appear at the bottom of a fucking chimney one day a year, as well.

The only thing I can tell you is that this is wrong. Money factors into nearly every decision that you make, when it should not even exist as anything more than a bartering chip. There is no medal to be won at the end of this marathon for the most tokens collected. We are all the same. We all have the same basic desires and needs.

As co-creators of our own realities, efforts are rewarded with the appropriate cause and effect energy that turns this entire earth around on its axis. If you want an abundance of anything in your life, visualize it, determine the actions necessary in order to create it, and follow through. It is that simple. This philosophy even applies to money. However, it is the abuse of, and intent to withhold money, that has placed us in dire straits.

The misconception that monetary and material abundance are only for a small and privileged population is a plague that has got our balls in a vice and about to burst. The boys in the club have manipulated the system to work in their favor; i.e. taking 30 percent of your earnings, failure prone loan structures, and inflated pricing. These are all methods of ensuring that you will be stuck in a cycle that is nearly impossible to break.

We are so distracted just trying to maintain a home, that we have forgotten our true nature and potential in this reality. Anything that you can imagine for yourself is possible. The current economic system has stripped away our imagination. We no longer dream of wild adventures, creating art, enjoying our loved ones and becoming great in our existence. We hope only to keep a roof over our heads and that some odd form of processed food is on our table in the evening.

You have been robbed of you. Somewhere buried beneath the credit cards, water bill, home loan, and tax return, your soul is begging to be remembered. Deep down you know that your life is not meant to be one long shift in the money mill. If you want to be a millionaire, you have every right to be a millionaire. We can all be millionaires. Money should never define you, but if the bartering tokens are what we have agreed upon as a form of exchange, then we all have a right to an abundance of tokens.

This will only happen when the stranglehold on our livelihood is released by the individuals and agencies that we naively give the idea of having some sort of power over our own lives. When we put money in its proper place at the center of the family table, it will flow freely from one end to the other.

As it stands now, it is as if we are at family game night and one or two of us are making up the rules as we go. These assholes create caveats and loopholes that have the flow of tokens trapped and bottle necked at various points around the board. They need to be spanked and sent to bed without dinner.

The Federal Reserve Bank is where the U.S. dollar is birthed into existence. This bank is by no means "Federal." The bank is a privately owned, and for profit business. For every dollar that they sell to the United States Government, they expect to be repaid with interest. Our ENTIRE economy is based upon one gigantic loan. There will forever be a national debt for as long as there are dollars in circulation. Every dollar in circulation represents a debt owed in the form of interest.

Do not misinterpret what I have just said as being a proponent for handouts and reward without effort. The universe does not operate on those principles anyhow. The flaw in our system lays in the fact that the chips are stacked. It is not a level playing field. Until it is, we will not be able to express ourselves to our full potential.

Each one of us is born with the right to have choices. No matter the neighborhood you grew up in, or the savings account your parents had. Money should never dictate what your imagination determines is possible for you.

8 IN A NUTSHELL

"It's not about what it is, it's about what it can become."

- Dr. Seuss, The Lorax

This book has been a short and wild ride. Like a Saturday night full of moonshine, your best friends, a midget, and a Polaroid camera, you may be left saying "Whoa, what the hell was that?" It's ok. I don't know if it is the point of our lives to ever have it all figured out. No one in history has succeeded thus far. Don't beat yourself up for not being the first.

I would like to think that we can all do our part to make this sleepover on earth an enjoyable one. All of the issues I have written about are just some things that seem to stand in the way of us having some fucking peace and equality every now and then. Most importantly, I hope to highlight the silliness of how seriously we take ourselves and the importance we place on "being right".

It was not my intent to provide any answers. I don't necessarily have them. I simply wanted to point out some huge, gaping, cavernous holes in our methods and processes that seem to be doing more harm than good.

You are as great of a leader, lover, philosopher and creator as any of the icons in our history. There is no magic "Jesus" gene, or predisposition towards being enlightened. Personally, I believe that there is just the realization that you can be whoever you want to be. I cannot begin to explain the universe and the way that it works. I just know that it is beyond awesome, and that is good enough for me.

If this book ends up as one minuscule battle cry for an awakening in this infinite human drama, then so be it. I tried. However, I've got to believe that maybe, just maybe, if we all shout at once, at the same time, that the earth could move and we would be off on one hell of a ride.

About the Author

You ever notice how the "About the Author" section of a book is always written in the third person? Kind of stupid considering that you know damn well the author wrote it about themselves.

Originally from the Pacific Northwest, I live in North County San Diego with my wife and two boys. She is beautiful and they are amazing. I am a Seattle soul with a San Diego heart. I have worked for years in aviation and enjoy getting dirty. My interests will never fit inside the confines of a paragraph. However, as long as my life involves my phenomenal family, great friends, outstanding food, and a whole lot of love...then it's all good.

I wrote this book because I love my life. I love living. I love being here, but I know that it can be even better. I know that I am not alone.

We all have a story to tell. We all have something great to give. I put mine into words. If yours is a song, a painting, a ten story building, or simply a life lived with grace – I hope that our stories cross paths. We are all co-authors of the greatest book there is. Life.

www.ingramcontent.com/pod-product-compliance
Lightning Source LLC
Chambersburg PA
CBHW061346040426
42444CB00011B/3113